THE COMP HEALTHY COOKBOOK

FOR TEEN CHEFS

**Mouth-Watering Recipes
Your Whole Family and Friends Will Love.
Essential Cooking Techniques to
Motivate and Inspire**

Britney Kim

TABLE OF CONTENTS

INTRODUCTION

Hello there! If you are reading this book, chances are you are a teen interested in learning to cook. Or maybe your parents, grandparents, friends, or someone else suggested that you learn to cook. Perhaps you want to become more independent and self-sufficient by learning to cook. Whatever the reason, look no further because this is the perfect book for you. I want to thank you for selecting this book before we get started. It will act as your guide every step of the way and turn you into a teen chef. If you are interested in blowing away your loved ones with delicious and simple home-cooked meals, you are in the right place.

If you are new to cooking or don't know your way around the kitchen, cooking probably sounds intimidating. After all, there are different cooking techniques, methods, appliances, and skills needed. There is much to do, from learning about the combination of spices and aromatics to cutting vegetables and cooking meat. So, before we begin, take a deep breath. Cooking is simple once you know what to do. Cooking is not complicated by any means. You will have a blast if you are willing to learn and don't mind experimenting in the kitchen! Also, cooking is quite a nice hobby and a relaxing activity. There is something incredibly satisfying about digging into a delicious meal you have cooked for yourself and your loved ones. What more? Knowing that your meals are healthy makes the entire experience even better.

Simply put, cooking is not only functional but fun too. It pleases your eyes, stomach, and soul at once. If you do it right, it is healthy!

Healthy is one word commonly used in most conversations, but people seldom know what it means. It often conjures images of diets, restrictions, and expensive, fancy, and exotic ingredients. Eating healthily is needed and is all the most important aspects of maintaining your health and well-being. Knowing that you are eating healthily will make you feel better. That said, this is one word that is quite confusing too. Perhaps you remember your mother sneaking healthy greens into your meals or disliking some especially healthy foods such as Brussels sprouts. Even if you have outgrown such things, understanding what healthy means is needed. So, how hard is it to cook healthily? Do I have to spend hours together in the kitchen to cook healthy meals? Is it difficult and expensive? Will I be able to do it? Chances are you are wondering about all these things. Well, cooking healthy meals at home is not only doable but also easy, affordable, and quick. Also, you don't have to be a natural or a pro in the kitchen to achieve this goal. This is where this book steps into the picture.

When it comes to cooking, learning the basics is needed. You should learn and master a couple of basic cooking techniques. Once you do this, the time spent cooking will automatically reduce. This book will act as your guide every step of the way. The different recipes in this book will introduce you to the most important and basic cooking techniques everyone must know. It forms the basis for healthy home cooking. An important component needed in cooking is creativity. After going through the information about basic cooking techniques and recipes, you will better understand what to do in the kitchen. This, in turn, will improve your confidence in the kitchen, making it easier to cook.

When cooking is sustainable, simple, interesting, applicable, easy to replicate, and uses wholesome ingredients, it automatically becomes healthy. When you start cooking at home and doing those mentioned above, the dependence on takeaways and processed and prepackaged foods reduces. This is not only good for your health but your bank balance too. After all, money saved is money earned. Cooking at home is certainly cheaper than eating out. It also gives you a better idea of where your food comes from. This, in turn, will improve your relationship with food. You can maintain food hygiene and safety while cooking at home. This means you can rest easy knowing you're giving your body all the nutrients it needs to function effectively and efficiently. Another benefit of home cooking is that it gives you complete control over portions and the quality of ingredients used. So, no more harmful additives, sugars, and preservatives in your meals. This also gives you flexibility.

Take a while and go through all the different recipes in this book. They are divided into different categories for your convenience. Go through them, note the ones that strike your fancy, and gather the needed ingredients. During the initial stages, stick to the recipes and after you get the hang of the cooking techniques, the combination of ingredients, and the process involved, feel free to experiment. Once you know the basics, there are no hard and fast rules about cooking. Instead, let your imagination run wild and experiment. To make things even easier, use the recipes in this book to make a weekly meal plan for yourself. Eating healthily also becomes easy when you know what and when you will eat. With a little planning and preparation, cooking becomes simple. You can use it to create a monthly budget too.

Now, let's not get ahead of ourselves; if you are excited to jump into the world of delicious and healthy home cooking, there is no time like the present to get started. Take a deep breath and take the first step. Let's start immediately!

WANT TO KNOW THE 7 PROVEN COOKING STRATEGIES FOR CHEFS?

GET IT NOW!

SIMPLY SCAN THIS QR CODE USING YOUR SMARTPHONE OR TABLET.

CHAPTER 1

SMOOTHIE RECIPES

STRAWBERRY BANANA BLAST

Servings: 2

NUTRITIONAL VALUES PER SERVING:
1 smoothie
Calories: 122
Fat: 1 g
Carbohydrate: 28 g
Protein: 3 g

INGREDIENTS:
- ½ cup orange juice
- ½ medium banana, sliced, frozen
- 1 cup frozen strawberries, unsweetened
- 6 tablespoons strawberry banana yogurt

DIRECTIONS:
1. Put all the ingredients in a high-speed blender. Blitz until smooth.
2. Pour into 2 glasses and serve

BLUEBERRY CHEESECAKE SMOOTHIE (VEGAN)

Servings: 2

NUTRITIONAL VALUES PER SERVING:
1 smoothie
Calories: 350
Fat: 11.7 g
Carbohydrate: 48 g
Protein: 15.9 g

INGREDIENTS:
- 2 cups frozen blueberries
- ⅔ cup extra-firm tofu
- 2 cups vanilla soy milk
- 1 banana, sliced, frozen
- 2 tablespoons cashews
- 1 teaspoon vanilla extract

DIRECTIONS:
1. Add blueberries, tofu, milk, banana, cashews, and vanilla into a blender. Blend for 30 – 40 seconds or until smooth.
2. Pour into 2 glasses and serve.

COPYCAT JAMBA JUICE BANANA BERRY SMOOTHIE

Servings: 1

NUTRITIONAL VALUES PER SERVING:
Calories: 302
Fat: 3 g
Carbohydrate: 38 g
Protein: 5 g

INGREDIENTS:
- ⅔ banana, sliced
- ⅔ cup raspberry sherbet
- ½ cup frozen blueberries
- ¼ cup fat-free frozen yogurt
- Ice cubes, as required
- 1/3 cup berry blend juice

DIRECTIONS:
1. Place banana, raspberry sherbet, blueberries, yogurt, ice cubes, and berry blend juice in a high-speed blender.
2. Blitz until smooth.
3. Pour into a glass and serve.

PEANUT BUTTER, JELLY, AND DATE SMOOTHIE (VEGAN)

Servings: 2

NUTRITIONAL VALUES PER SERVING:
1 smoothie
Calories: 374
Fat: 13 g
Carbohydrate: 60 g
Protein: 8 g

INGREDIENTS:
- 8 dates, pitted
- 2 medium bananas, sliced, frozen
- ⅔ cup blueberries
- 2 tablespoons natural peanut butter
- 1 ½ cups vanilla almond milk, unsweetened
- 2 tablespoons flaxseed meal

DIRECTIONS:
1. Place dates, bananas, blueberries, peanut butter, milk, and flaxseeds in a blender. Blend for 30 – 40 seconds or until smooth.
2. Pour into 2 glasses and serve.

PEACHY KEEN SMOOTHIE

Servings: 2

NUTRITIONAL VALUES PER SERVING:
1 smoothie
Calories: 118
Fat: 1 g
Carbohydrate: 25 g
Protein: 3 g

INGREDIENTS:
- 8 ounces frozen peach slices
- ½ cup peach juice
- ½ cup frozen yogurt
- ½ banana, sliced

DIRECTIONS:
1. Place peach, peach juice, yogurt, and banana in a high-speed blender.
2. Blitz until smooth.
3. Pour into 2 glasses and serve.

VANILLA CLEMENTINE PROTEIN SMOOTHIE (VEGAN)

Servings: 2

NUTRITIONAL VALUES PER SERVING:
1 smoothie
Calories: 336
Fat: 11.1 g
Carbohydrate: 39.8 g
Protein: 27.3 g

INGREDIENTS:
- 6 clementines, peeled, separated into segments, deseeded
- 2 cups light vanilla soy milk
- 16 almonds
- 1 scoop of vegan vanilla protein powder
- 2 tablespoons flaxseed meal
- Ice cubes, as required

DIRECTIONS:
1. Place clementines, milk, almonds, protein powder, flaxseed meal, and ice cubes in a blender. Blend for 30 – 40 seconds or until smooth.
2. Pour into 2 glasses and serve.

HEALTHY CHOCOLATE PROTEIN SHAKE

Servings: 1

NUTRITIONAL VALUES PER SERVING:
Calories: 250
Fat: 9 g
Carbohydrate: 38 g
Protein: 10 g

INGREDIENTS:
- ¾ cup almond milk
- 2 large dates, pitted
- 1 tablespoon cocoa powder
- A pinch of ground cinnamon
- ½ cup frozen organic kale
- 1 tablespoon hemp seeds, hulled
- 1 medium banana, sliced, frozen
- ⅛ cup chopped avocado
- Ice cubes, as required

DIRECTIONS:
1. Add milk, dates, cocoa, cinnamon kale, hemp seeds, banana, avocado, and ice into a blender. Blend for 30 – 40 seconds or until smooth.
2. Pour into a glass and serve.

CHAPTER 2

BREAKFAST RECIPES

BOILED EGGS / POACHED EGGS

Servings: 1

NUTRITIONAL VALUES PER SERVING:
1 egg
Calories: 72
Fat: 4.7 g
Carbohydrate: 0.4 g
Protein: 6.3 g

INGREDIENTS:
- 1 egg
- Water, as required
- 1 teaspoon vinegar (for poached egg)

DIRECTIONS:
1. Place a small pot filled with water over high heat. When the water begins to boil, turn down the heat to low. Place the egg on a spoon. Carefully lower the egg into the pot. You can boil more eggs if desired.
2. For soft-boiled eggs: Cook for 4-5 minutes, depending on the size of the egg (medium or large).
3. For medium-boiled eggs: Cook for 7-8 minutes, depending on the size of the egg.
4. For hard-boiled eggs: Cook for 8-10 minutes, depending on the size of the egg.
5. Drain and add chilled water into the pot when the eggs are cooked, as you like.
6. Peel after 4-5 minutes and use as required.

7. To poach eggs: Boil a pan of water over high heat. When the water starts boiling, turn down the heat to medium heat. Stir in the vinegar.

8. Break the egg into a tiny cup or bowl. Stir the water using a spoon and carefully slide the egg into the water. Let it simmer for about 3 to 4 minutes, depending on how you like the egg to be cooked. You will see a film over the yolk, and the white will be set.

9. If you have to poach more than one egg, repeat the previous step for each egg. You should add only one egg into a cup each time, but you can poach 2 – 3 eggs at a time if your pan is large enough.

10. Remove the egg with a slotted spoon. Hold the spoon over the simmering water to drop off any water from the egg.

11. Serve garnished with salt and pepper or any other seasoning of your choice.

BASIC FRIED EGGS

Servings: 4

NUTRITIONAL VALUES PER SERVING:
1 fried egg
Calories: 132
Fat: 11.8 g
Carbohydrate: 0.4 g
Protein: 6.3 g

INGREDIENTS:
- 4 eggs
- Salt to taste
- Pepper to taste
- 4 tablespoons extra-virgin olive oil

DIRECTIONS:
1. Place a nonstick pan over medium heat. Add 1 tablespoon of oil. When the oil is hot, crack an egg into a bowl and carefully slide it into the pan.
2. For sunny side up: Cook until the white is set and the yolk is runny.
3. For over-easy: When the white is set, flip the side once. Cook for about 30 seconds.
4. For over-medium: When the white is set, flip the side once. Cook for about 60-100 seconds.
5. For over-hard: When the white is set, flip the side once. Cook for 2-3 minutes or until the yolk is cooked well, like a hard-boiled egg.
6. For steam-fried eggs: Cook the eggs sunny side up (step 2) but cover the pan with a lid when the whites are lightly set.
7. 7. Season the eggs with salt and pepper and serve them hot once they are cooked to your preference. Cook the remaining eggs similarly.

SOFT AND CREAMY SCRAMBLED EGGS

Servings: 2

NUTRITIONAL VALUES PER SERVING:
½ recipe
Calories: 179
Fat: 13.4 g
Carbohydrate: 1 g
Protein: 13 g

INGREDIENTS:
- 4 large eggs
- 2 teaspoons butter
- Salt to taste
- ½ teaspoon freshly cracked pepper or to taste (optional)

DIRECTIONS:
1. Crack eggs into a bowl. Add salt and whisk lightly until well combined.
2. Place a nonstick pan over medium heat. Add butter and let it melt. Add the egg mixture. Do not stir for 20 seconds.
3. Using a silicone spatula, stir lightly in small circles for 30 seconds until slightly curdled.
4. Stir in bigger circles for the next 15 to 20 seconds until the egg is curdy in texture. The eggs should be soft yet set and runny in a few places. If the eggs are getting cooked too quickly, take the pan off the heat for a few seconds and keep stirring.
5. Turn off the heat. Let it cook in the heat for 8-10 seconds.
6. Stir lightly. Serve right away after adding additional salt and pepper to taste.

COPYCAT TACO BELL BREAKFAST CRUNCH WRAP

Servings: 4

NUTRITIONAL VALUES PER SERVING:
1 crunch wrap
Calories: 480
Fat: 31 g
Carbohydrate: 28 g
Protein: 21 g

INGREDIENTS:
- 4 flour tortillas
- 4 tablespoons shredded cheddar cheese
- 8 tablespoons taco bell sauce
- 6 eggs
- Salt to taste
- 1 cup hash browns or 4 fried hash brown patties
- 8 slices bacon, cooked until crisp
- Pepper to taste

DIRECTIONS:
1. Place a nonstick pan over medium heat. Spray some cooking spray. Follow the previous recipe to make the scrambled eggs (here, cooking oil spray is used instead of butter).
2. Warm the tortillas following the instructions given on the package of tortillas.
3. Divide equally and spread the hash browns on the tortillas, or place one hash brown patty on each.
4. Divide the eggs, taco bell sauce, and cheese equally among the tortillas. Scatter bacon on top.
5. Fold the side that is nearest to you over the filling. Next, fold the other 2 edges (left and right) over the filling. Finally, fold the last side over the center.
6. Place a nonstick skillet over medium heat.
7. Place a filled wrap in the pan. Cook until crisp and golden brown on both sides.
8. Repeat the process with the remaining tortillas.

CRANBERRY CORNMEAL MUFFINS

Servings: 6

NUTRITIONAL VALUES PER SERVING:
1 muffin
Calories: 269
Fat: 10 g
Carbohydrate: 41 g
Protein: 5 g

INGREDIENTS:
- 4 tablespoons unsalted butter, cut into pieces
- ½ cup yellow cornmeal
- ½ teaspoon baking soda
- ¼ cup sugar
- 10 tablespoons plain yogurt
- ⅛ teaspoon maple extract (optional)
- 1 cup all-purpose flour
- ¾ teaspoon baking powder
- ¼ teaspoon salt
- 2 tablespoons maple syrup
- 1 large egg
- ¾ cup fresh or frozen cranberries

DIRECTIONS:
1. Preheat the oven to 400° F. Take a muffin pan of 6 counts. You can also use 6 muffin cups. Now brush some oil into the muffin cups. You can also spray cooking oil into the cups instead of brushing the oil. Place disposable paper liners in the cups if you have any at home.
2. Add flour, baking soda, baking powder, flour, and salt into a mixing bowl and stir until the mixture is well combined.

3. Add butter to a microwave-safe bowl. Place the bowl in the microwave and melt the butter for about 20 – 30 seconds.
4. Add sugar and maple syrup into the bowl of butter and whisk until well incorporated.
5. Add egg, yogurt, and maple extract and continue whisking until smooth and well incorporated.
6. Next, you have to pour the butter mixture into the mixing bowl with flour.
7. Stir until just combined. Make sure you do not over-mix.
8. Add cranberries and fold gently until the cranberries are distributed in the batter.
9. Spoon the batter into the muffin cups. Fill the cups up to ⅔.
10. Place the muffin cups in the oven. Make sure to wear oven mitts. Set the timer for about 18 minutes. Let them bake until they look golden brown on top and cook through inside.
11. To check if the muffins are cooked, take a toothpick and insert it in the center of a muffin. Now take out the toothpick and check if there is any batter stuck on the toothpick. If you find any batter, you have to bake it for a few more minutes.
12. Once the muffins are baked, take them out and let them cool for 5 – 8 minutes in the muffin pan.
13. Take out the muffins and set them on a wire rack.
14. You can serve them warm or at room temperature.

WHOLE-WHEAT PANCAKES

Servings: 5

NUTRITIONAL VALUES PER SERVING:
2 pancakes, without toppings
Calories: 157
Fat: 4 g
Carbohydrate: 24 g
Protein: 9 g

INGREDIENTS:
- 1 cup whole wheat flour
- ½ teaspoon baking soda
- ¼ cup toasted wheat germ
- ¼ teaspoon salt
- 1 ½ cups buttermilk
- 1 large egg at room temperature
- ½ tablespoon canola oil
- Cooking oil spray

DIRECTIONS:
1. Add flour, baking soda, wheat germ, and salt into a bowl and stir.
2. If you do not have buttermilk, take 1-½ cups of milk and add a tablespoon of vinegar. Stir well and set it aside for 20 minutes. The milk will sort of curdle. Well, this can be used instead of buttermilk.
3. Add butter, milk, egg, and oil into another bowl and whisk well. Pour the buttermilk mixture into the bowl of the flour mixture and stir until just combined, making sure not to over-mix.
4. Place a nonstick pan over medium heat. Spray the pan with some cooking oil spray. When the pan is hot, pour ¼ cup of batter on the pan. In a while, bubbles will appear on the top. Cook until the underside is golden brown. Cook the opposite side of the pancake by flipping it. Remove the pancake onto a plate and keep it warm.
5. Repeat the process with the remaining batter.
6. Serve with toppings of your choice.

BLACKBERRIES AND CREAM STUFFED FRENCH TOAST

Servings: 2

NUTRITIONAL VALUES PER SERVING:
2 French toasts
Calories: 667
Fat: 29 g
Carbohydrate: 78 g
Protein: 23 g

INGREDIENTS:
- ½ loaf of French bread, cut into 8 slices (½ inch each)
- 2 tablespoons sugar
- ¼ cup heavy cream
- ¼ teaspoon almond extract
- 3 small eggs
- 6 tablespoons milk
- ½ teaspoon vanilla extract

For the filling:
- 2 ounces cream cheese, softened
- ½ cup fresh blackberries
- ½ teaspoon sugar
- Cooking oil spray or butter for cooking

DIRECTIONS:
1. To prepare the bread: If you have a couple of days old bread, use that and skip the next step.
2. Lay the bread slices on a baking sheet and place them in the oven (do not preheat the oven). Set the temperature of the oven to 350° F. Turn the oven on. When the oven temperature

touches 350° F, check if the bread is dried. If it is dried, take out the baking sheet or bake for a couple of minutes until the bread is dried.

3. Crack eggs into a bowl. Add sugar, almond extract, vanilla extract, cream, and milk into a bowl and beat until smooth.

4. To make the filling: Combine berries and sugar in a bowl and mash them up. Spread ½ ounce of cream cheese on each of the four bread slices. Spread the berries over the cream cheese layer.

5. Now place the other bread slices over the berry layer. So now you have 4 berry stuffed sandwiches.

6. Next, place a nonstick pan over medium heat. Spray some cooking spray or add a little butter to the pan.

7. Lift a blueberry sandwich and dip it in the egg mixture. Both sides should be coated in the egg mixture. Lift it and shake off excess. Place the sandwich in the pan. Repeat the same process with the other 3 sandwiches.

8. Cook until the underside is golden brown. Turn the sandwich over and cook the other side as well.

9. Serve warm. You can garnish with some cream or blackberries if desired.

MCDONALD'S STYLE BREAKFAST BURRITO

Servings: 2

NUTRITIONAL VALUES PER SERVING:
1 burrito
Calories: 353
Fat: 24 g
Carbohydrate: 14.5 g
Protein: 20.2 g

INGREDIENTS:
- 2 eggs
- ¼ pound sausage
- ½ tablespoon petite diced tomatoes, diced once again
- 2 tortillas
- Salsa or Picante sauce to garnish
- 2 tablespoons skim milk
- 1 teaspoon minced onion
- ½ tablespoon canned green chilies
- 2 slices American cheese, halved
- Butter, to cook the eggs

DIRECTIONS:
1. Whisk eggs and skim milk in a bowl.
2. Place sausage in a pan. Place the pan over medium-low heat and cook until light brown. As you stir, break the sausage into smaller crumbles.
3. Stir in tomatoes, onion, and green chilies. Cook for a couple of minutes. Remove the pan from heat.
4. Place another pan over medium heat. Add butter and wait for it to melt.

5. Crack the eggs into the pan. Stir on and off. Cook the eggs to the desired doneness. Turn off the heat.
6. To assemble: Warm the tortilla following the instructions given on the package.
7. Stack 2 cheese halves on each tortilla and place them along the diameter of the tortilla. Divide the sausage mixture among the tortillas and place it over the cheese slices.
8. Divide the scrambled egg equally and place it over the sausage. Fold the left and right sides inwards over a part of the filling. Now lift the side nearest to you, and place it over the filling. Start rolling it along with the filling until you reach the other end. This is how you fold a burrito. Place it with the seam side facing down.
9. Serve.

YOGURT AND HONEY FRUIT CUPS

Servings: 3

NUTRITIONAL VALUES PER SERVING:
¾ cup
Calories: 97
Fat: 0.5 g
Carbohydrate: 23 g
Protein: 2 g

INGREDIENTS:
- 2 ¼ cups chopped fresh fruit of your choice
- ½ tablespoon honey
- ⅛ teaspoon almond extract
- 6 tablespoons orange or vanilla yogurt
- ¼ teaspoon grated orange peel

DIRECTIONS:
1. Take 3 serving bowls and distribute the fruits among the bowls.
2. Whisk together honey, yogurt, almond extract, and orange peel in a bowl.
3. Divide equally and drizzle over the fruits.
4. Serve.

SAVORY CHEESE MUFFINS

Servings: 22

NUTRITIONAL VALUES PER SERVING:
1 muffin
Calories: 275
Fat: 18 g
Carbohydrate: 20 g
Protein: 8.1 g

INGREDIENTS:
- 6 tablespoons salted butter
- 4 cups grated cheddar cheese
- 4 cloves garlic, peeled, minced, crushed
- 4 cups all-purpose flour
- 1 teaspoon baking soda
- 3 teaspoons baking powder
- 1 teaspoon salt
- 2 cups milk
- 3 tablespoons vegetable oil
- 2 cloves garlic, peeled, crushed
- 2 large eggs, lightly beaten
- ½ cup sour cream or plain yogurt
- ½ cup minced chopped fresh parsley

DIRECTIONS:
1. Set the oven temperature to 350 º F and preheat the oven.
2. Combine minced garlic and butter in a microwave-safe container and melt it in a microwave for about 20 to 30 seconds.

3. Brush this mixture into 22 muffin cups of 2 muffin pans of 12 counts each. Make sure each hole has a bit of garlic in it. Do not use all of it; keep some to use later.
4. 4. In a bowl, mash together the flour, salt, baking soda, and baking powder.
5. Combine milk, oil, crushed garlic, eggs, yogurt, and parsley in another bowl.
6. Add the milk mixture into the bowl of the flour mixture and stir until well combined.
7. Add cheese and fold until just combined. Spoon the batter into the muffin cups. Fill up to ¾ the muffin cups.
8. Place the muffin pans in the oven and set the timer for about 25 minutes or until golden brown and firm on top.
9. Take out the muffins from the pans and place them on a cooling rack. Brush the butter garlic mixture on top, which was set aside.

CHAPTER 3

SOUP
RECIPES

CHICKEN AND WHITE BEAN SOUP

Servings: 3

NUTRITIONAL VALUES PER SERVING:
1-½ cups
Calories: 248
Fat: 5.8 g
Carbohydrate: 14.8 g
Protein: 35.1 g

INGREDIENTS:
- 1 teaspoon extra-virgin olive oil
- ½ tablespoon chopped fresh sage or ⅛ teaspoon dried sage
- 1 cup water
- 2 cups roasted, shredded chicken (skinless, boneless)
- 1 leek, cut into ¼-inch thick slices (white and light green parts)
- 1 can (14 ounces) of chicken broth
- ½ can (from 15 ounces can) cannellini beans, rinsed
- Salt to taste
- Pepper to taste

DIRECTIONS:
1. Place a soup pot or Dutch oven over medium-high heat. Pour oil into the pot and let it heat. Once the oil is hot, add leeks and stir on and off for a couple of minutes or until tender.
2. Add sage and cook for a few more seconds until you get a pleasant aroma.
3. Add broth and water and stir. Cover the pot and let it cook for about 5 minutes.
4. When the mixture starts boiling, stir in the beans and chicken. Stir on and off and let the soup heat thoroughly. Add salt and pepper to taste.
5. Ladle into soup bowls and serve.

PEA SOUP

Servings: 3

NUTRITIONAL VALUES PER SERVING:
1 cup, without toppings
Calories: 126
Fat: 3 g
Carbohydrate: 19 g
Protein: 7 g

INGREDIENTS:
- ½ cup water
- 1 teaspoon canola oil or any cooking oil
- 5 ounces frozen peas
- ¼ teaspoon salt
- ¼ cup quinoa, rinsed
- ½ medium onion, chopped
- 1 can (14 ounces) of chicken broth or vegetable broth
- Pepper to taste

Optional toppings:
- Yogurt
- Sour cream
- Croutons
- Parmesan cheese
- Any other toppings of your choice

DIRECTIONS:

1. Pour ½ cup of water into a small saucepan. Place the saucepan over medium-high heat.
2. When the water starts boiling, stir in the quinoa.
3. Turn down the heat and cover the saucepan with a lid. Cook until there is no water left in the saucepan. It should take around 10 minutes. Turn off the heat.
4. Pour canola oil into a saucepan and place the saucepan over medium-high heat.
5. When the oil is hot, add onion and cook until soft.
6. Add broth and peas. When the broth starts boiling, turn down the heat and cook until they are tender.
7. Add quinoa and stir. Cut the heat off. The soup should be smooth after being pureed using an immersion blender. Add salt and pepper to taste.
8. Ladle into soup bowls and serve with desired toppings.

COPYCAT CHILI'S STYLE SOUTHWEST CHICKEN SOUP

Servings: 4

NUTRITIONAL VALUES PER SERVING:
¼ recipe without optional toppings
Calories: 173
Fat: 7 g
Carbohydrate: 12 g
Protein: 16 g

INGREDIENTS:
- ½ pound boneless chicken breast
- ½ cup chopped onion
- 1 tablespoon vegetable oil
- 2 cups chicken stock
- ½ cup white hominy
- ½ cup diced tomatoes
- ½ teaspoon minced garlic
- ¼ cup chopped celery
- ½ tablespoon tomato paste
- ½ teaspoon chipotle peppers in adobo sauce or more to taste
- 2 ounces canned green chilies, sliced

Optional toppings:
- Fried corn tortilla strips
- Chopped cilantro
- Grated cheese
- Lime juice to taste

DIRECTIONS:

1. Pour ½ tablespoon oil into a soup pot. Place the pot over medium heat and let it heat.
2. Sprinkle salt over the chicken and place it in the pot. Cook for about 6 to 7 minutes. When the chicken is thoroughly done inside, flip it over and cook the second side for 6 to 7 minutes.
3. Take the chicken from the pot and place it on your cutting board. When it cools slightly, shred the chicken with a pair of forks.
4. Pour ½ tablespoon oil into the soup pot. When the oil is heated, add onion and garlic and cook until the onion turns soft.
5. Stir in celery and cook for about 2 – 3 minutes. Stir in the tomato paste. Stir constantly for about 30 – 40 seconds.
6. Stir in broth, chipotle pepper, tomatoes, green chilies, and hominy.
7. Add the chicken to the pot. Give the soup a good stir. Heat thoroughly.
8. Add lime juice and stir. Turn off the heat.
9. Ladle into soup bowls. Sprinkle cilantro and cheese on top. Scatter fried tortilla strips on top and serve.

SPICY PUMPKIN AND CORN SOUP

Servings: 4

NUTRITIONAL VALUES PER SERVING:
¾ cup
Calories: 100
Fat: 0 g
Carbohydrate: 20 g
Protein: 6 g

INGREDIENTS:
- ½ can (from 15 ounces can) of pumpkin
- ¾ cup frozen corn
- 1 can (14 ounces) of low-sodium chicken broth or vegetable broth
- ½ can (from a 15-ounce can) of black beans, rinsed, drained
- ½ can (from 10 ounces can) of diced tomatoes with green chilies
- Pepper to taste

DIRECTIONS:
1. Add pumpkin, corn, broth, black beans, tomatoes, and pepper into a saucepan.
2. Place the saucepan over medium heat. Stir often. When the soup starts boiling, turn down the heat and let it boil gently for about 10 minutes or until the soup is slightly thick.
3. Ladle into soup bowls and serve.

MINESTRONE SOUP

Servings: 4

NUTRITIONAL VALUES PER SERVING:
¼ recipe
Calories: 204
Fat: 4 g
Carbohydrate: 34 g
Protein: 10 g

INGREDIENTS:
- 1 tablespoon olive oil
- ¼ cup diced celery
- ½ zucchini, diced
- ½ can (from 14 ounces can) of diced tomatoes
- 2 small bay leaves
- 1 tablespoon tomato paste
- ½ can (from 15 ounces can) of kidney beans, drained, rinsed
- ½ can (from a 15-ounce can) of small white beans, drained, rinsed
- ½ cup fresh or frozen beans
- Chopped parsley to garnish
- ½ cup chopped onion
- ¼ cup peeled, diced carrots
- 1 teaspoon minced garlic
- 2 cups vegetable stock
- 1 tablespoon tomato paste
- ¼ cup small shell-shaped pasta
- Salt to taste

DIRECTIONS:

1. This soup tastes as good as the one you get at Olive Garden.
2. Pour oil into a soup pot or saucepan and place it over medium heat. When the oil is hot, add onion, garlic, carrots, and celery and mix well.
3. Add a bit of salt and mix well. Cook until the vegetables are slightly tender.
4. Stir in tomatoes, tomato paste, broth, bay leaves, and Italian seasoning.
5. When the soup starts boiling, turn down the heat to low. Stir in zucchini, pasta, kidney beans, green beans, and white beans, and let it simmer for about 15 minutes or until the vegetables and pasta are tender.
6. Ladle into soup bowls and serve.

COPYCAT PANERA BREAD BLACK BEAN SOUP

Servings: 4

NUTRITIONAL VALUES PER SERVING:
¼ recipe
Calories: 192
Fat: 4 g
Carbohydrate: 30 g
Protein: 9 g

INGREDIENTS:
- ½ cup chopped onion
- ¼ cup chopped carrot
- ¼ cup chopped red bell pepper
- ¼ cup chopped celery
- 1 tablespoon vegetable oil
- 1 teaspoon minced garlic
- 2 cups cooked or canned black beans
- ½ - 1 teaspoon ground cumin
- ½ tablespoon cornstarch mixed with 2 tablespoons of water
- Salt to taste
- 2 cups vegetable stock
- 1 teaspoon lemon juice or to taste

DIRECTIONS:
1. Pour 1 tablespoon of oil into a pot and place the pot over high heat.
2. Add celery, onion, and carrots when the oil is hot and mix well. Add a pinch of salt and mix well.
3. Cook until the vegetables are slightly tender. Stir often.
4. Stir in black beans, about ½ teaspoon salt, stock, and ground cumin. Let the soup heat thoroughly.
5. Add the cornstarch mixture and constantly stir until the soup is thick.
6. Turn off the heat. The lemon juice is to be added just before you serve.
7. Ladle the soup into bowls and serve.

ROASTED RED PEPPER AND CHICKPEAS SOUP

Servings: 4

NUTRITIONAL VALUES PER SERVING:
2 cups
Calories: 488
Fat: 8 g
Carbohydrate: 78 g
Protein: 26 g

INGREDIENTS:
- 2 cartons (32 ounces each) of roasted red pepper soup
- 6 cups baby spinach
- 2 cans (15 ounces each) of unsalted chickpeas, rinsed, drained

DIRECTIONS:
1. Pour roasted red pepper soup into a soup pot or saucepan. Place the pot over medium heat.
2. When the soup starts boiling, add the chickpeas. Let the soup start boiling once again.
3. Add spinach and cook for about 2 minutes. Turn off the heat.
4. Ladle the soup into bowls. Sprinkle some freshly cracked pepper on top (optional) and serve.

CHAPTER 4

SALAD

RECIPES

WATERMELON SALAD

Servings: 4

NUTRITIONAL VALUES PER SERVING:
¾ cup
Calories: 56
Fat: 2 g
Carbohydrate: 9 g
Protein: 1 g

INGREDIENTS:
- 3 cups cubed, deseeded watermelon
- ½ tablespoon lemon juice
- 1 teaspoon sugar
- 1 tablespoon minced fresh mint
- ½ tablespoon olive oil

DIRECTIONS:
1. Add lemon juice, sugar, and oil into a bowl and whisk until the sugar dissolves completely.
2. Add watermelon and mint and stir lightly.
3. Serve.

CLASSIC CHICKEN SALAD

Servings: 2

NUTRITIONAL VALUES PER SERVING:
½ recipe
Calories: 388
Fat: 18 g
Carbohydrate: 19 g
Protein: 37 g

INGREDIENTS:
For the salad:
- ½ pound raw chicken
- ¼ red bell pepper, cut into ½ inch squares
- ⅛ cup chopped red onion
- 2 cups chopped lettuce
- 1 rib celery, chopped
- 2 – 3 green olives, pitted, minced
- ½ cup chopped apple

For the dressing:
- 2 ½ tablespoons mayonnaise
- 1 teaspoon fresh lemon juice or to taste
- ½ tablespoon plum preserves or any other sweet berry preserve or honey or more to taste
- Pepper to taste
- Salt to taste

DIRECTIONS:

1. *How to cook chicken:* Place the chicken in a stockpot. Cover with cold water. Sprinkle salt.
2. Place the stockpot over medium heat. Boil until the chicken is cooked through. Turn off the heat. Cover the pot and let it rest for 10 minutes. With a pair of tongs, remove the chicken and shred, chop, or use it as needed. You can use the cooked water as chicken stock in any recipe that needs it.
3. *To make the dressing:* Combine mayonnaise, lemon juice, preserves, pepper, and salt in a bowl.
4. Add bell pepper, onion, celery, olives, apple, and chicken into the bowl and stir until well combined.
5. Chill until use. Add lettuce just before serving. Fold gently and serve.

BALSAMIC CUCUMBER SALAD

Servings: 3

NUTRITIONAL VALUES PER SERVING:
¾ cup
Calories: 90
Fat: 5 g
Carbohydrate: 9 g
Protein: 4 g

INGREDIENTS:
- ½ large cucumber, halved lengthwise, sliced crosswise
- ½ medium red onion, thinly sliced
- 6 tablespoons crumbled reduced-fat feta cheese
- 1 cup grape tomatoes, halved
- ¼ cup balsamic vinaigrette

DIRECTIONS:
1. Add tomatoes, cucumber, and onion into a bowl and toss well.
2. Drizzle the vinaigrette over the vegetables and toss well.
3. Cover the bowl and chill until ready to serve.
4. Add cheese just before serving. Stir lightly and serve.

CALIFORNIAN AVOCADO SALAD

Servings: 4

NUTRITIONAL VALUES PER SERVING:
½ cup
Calories: 135
Fat: 11 g
Carbohydrate: 10 g
Protein: 2 g

INGREDIENTS:
For salad:

- 1 ½ medium oranges, peeled, separated into segments
- 1 medium ripe avocado, peeled, sliced
- 1 teaspoon minced fresh rosemary
- ⅛ cup toasted pine nuts
- ¼ cup salad leaves

For dressing:

- 2 tablespoons fat-free plain yogurt
- 2 tablespoons low-fat mayonnaise
- 1 tablespoon orange juice
- ½ teaspoon grated orange zest
- White pepper to taste
- 1 teaspoon honey
- ⅛ teaspoon salt

DIRECTIONS:

1. *To make the dressing:* Whisk together all the dressing ingredients in a bowl.
2. Cover the bowl and chill for a couple of hours for the flavors to meld.
3. *To make the salad:* Place oranges, salad leaves and avocado on a serving platter.
4. Scatter rosemary and pine nuts. Spoon the dressing all over the fruits and serve.

BACON CAULIFLOWER SALAD

Servings: 2

NUTRITIONAL VALUES PER SERVING:
½ recipe
Calories: 183.5
Fat: 16.23 g
Carbohydrate: 5.95 g
Protein: 4.96 g

INGREDIENTS:
- ¼ head cauliflower and broccoli, cut into florets
- ⅛ teaspoon salt
- 2 tablespoons olive oil
- ½ cup chopped parsley
- ½ red bell pepper, diced
- ¼ cup + ⅛ cup crumbled crispy bacon
- A pinch of black pepper
- 1 tablespoon lemon juice
- ½ small onion, chopped

DIRECTIONS:
1. *How to cook crispy bacon:* Set the oven temperature to 400 ⁰ F and preheat the oven. Prepare a baking sheet and line it with parchment paper.
2. Take about 8 slices of bacon and place them on the baking sheet next to each other.
3. Bake the baking sheet in the oven for 18 to 20 minutes, or until the food is crunchy.
4. Take out the baking sheet and place it on your countertop.
5. Line a plate with paper towels. Pick the bacon with a pair of tongs and place it on the plate. Let it cool completely. Now crumble the bacon. Use as much as required and store the remaining, if any, in an airtight container and use it in some other recipe.

6. Grate the cauliflower with a box grater and put it into a bowl. Add salt and pepper and toss well.

7. *To make the dressing:* Add lemon juice, oil, salt, and pepper to a small jar. Fasten the lid and shake the jar vigorously until well combined.

8. *To make the salad:* Combine bacon, onion, parsley, and bell pepper in a bowl. Add to the bowl of cauliflower. Toss well. Add dressing and toss well. Serve.

SPINACH SALAD WITH MOZZARELLA, TOMATO AND PEPPERONI

Servings: 2

NUTRITIONAL VALUES PER SERVING:
½ recipe
Calories: 321
Fat: 22.6 g
Carbohydrate: 18.7 g
Protein: 13.87 g

INGREDIENTS:
For the salad:

- 1 ½ cups baby spinach, roughly chopped
- ¼ small red onion, minced
- Chopped pepperoni or salami slices to taste
- 4 ounces assorted cherry or grape tomatoes, halved
- ¾ cup diced mozzarella cheese

For the dressing:

- 2 tablespoons olive oil
- Salt to taste
- 1 teaspoon lemon juice or white wine vinegar
- ¼ teaspoon Italian seasoning

DIRECTIONS:
1. To make the dressing: Add oil, salt, lemon juice, and Italian seasoning to a small jar. Fasten the lid and constantly shake for about a minute.
2. Add pepperoni, spinach, onion, tomatoes, and cheese into a bowl and toss well.
3. Add dressing and toss once again.
4. You can serve it right away or chill and serve it later.

WANT TO KNOW THE 7 PROVEN COOKING STRATEGIES FOR CHEFS?

GET IT NOW!

SIMPLY SCAN THIS QR CODE USING YOUR SMARTPHONE OR TABLET.

CHAPTER 5

LUNCH RECIPES

SWEET POTATO AND BEAN QUESADILLAS

Servings: 2

NUTRITIONAL VALUES PER SERVING:
1 quesadilla and 3 tablespoons salsa
Calories: 306
Fat: 8 g
Carbohydrate: 46 g
Protein: 11 g

INGREDIENTS:
- 1 medium sweet potato, scrubbed
- 6 tablespoons canned or cooked black beans, rinsed, drained
- 6 tablespoons salsa
- 2 whole-wheat tortillas (8 inches each)
- ¼ cup shredded pepper Jack cheese

DIRECTIONS:
1. Prick the sweet potato at different places using a fork. Place it in a microwave-safe bowl.
2. Place the bowl in the microwave. Set the microwave on high and timer for about 8 minutes. Cook until the sweet potato is cooked through inside. If you pierce a fork into the sweet potato, it should get in easily. If it gets in easily, the sweet potato is cooked; otherwise, cook for a couple of minutes longer.
3. Let the sweet potato cool for a while. Cut it into 2 halves. With a spoon, remove the sweet potato pulp. Spread the pulp on one-half of each tortilla.
4. Distribute the beans and cheese equally and place them over the sweet potato.
5. Lift the other half of the tortilla and place it over the filling such that it is over the edge of the tortilla. Press the tortilla. So now, the quesadilla will be in the shape of a semicircle. Do this with the other tortilla as well.

6. Place a skillet over medium heat. Place the quesadilla in the pan and cook until the underside is golden brown. Turn the quesadilla over and cook the other side until golden brown.
7. Remove onto a plate. Cut into wedges and serve.
8. Cook the other quesadilla in a similar manner.

CHICKEN QUINOA BOWL

Servings: 4

NUTRITIONAL VALUES PER SERVING:
1 bowl
Calories: 516
Fat: 27 g
Carbohydrate: 29 g
Protein: 43 g

INGREDIENTS:
- 1 boneless, skinless chicken breast half, cut into cubes
- ¼ cup dry quinoa
- ½ small avocado, sliced
- 1 large egg, soft boiled
- ½ tablespoon olive oil
- ½ cup water
- 1 cup arugula
- ¼ cup cherry tomatoes halved
- ½ tablespoon sesame seeds
- Salt to taste
- Pepper to taste

DIRECTIONS:
1. *To cook quinoa:* Pour water into a saucepan and place the saucepan over medium heat.
2. When the water starts boiling, stir in the quinoa. Cover the saucepan with a lid.
3. Turn down the heat to low heat and cook until no water remains in the saucepan.
4. While the quinoa is cooking, pour oil into a skillet and place the skillet over medium heat on another burner.
5. *To cook chicken:* Place chicken in a bowl. Sprinkle salt and pepper over the chicken and toss well.

6. Transfer the chicken to the skillet and give it a good stir. Now do not disturb the chicken for 2 – 3 minutes or until the underside is brown. Now flip sides and cook the other side until brown. Make sure it is brown all over.
7. Take the skillet off the heat and keep it aside for now.
8. Boiling the egg recipe is given in the Breakfast Chapter.
9. Peel the egg and cut it into 2 halves lengthwise.
10. *To assemble:* Take 2 bowls and divide the quinoa among the bowls. Divide the arugula, tomatoes, chicken, and avocado equally among the bowls. Sprinkle sesame seeds on top. Place an egg on top of each bowl and serve.

CHICKPEA AND TUNA LETTUCE WRAPS

Servings: 4

NUTRITIONAL VALUES PER SERVING:
3 wraps
Calories: 324
Fat: 9 g
Carbohydrate: 33 g
Protein: 30 g

INGREDIENTS:
- 2 cups cooked or canned chickpeas, drained, rinsed
- 12 butter lettuce leaves
- 2 small red onions, chopped
- 2 stalks of celery, chopped
- ¼ cup chopped cilantro
- Juice of 2 lemons
- 2 tablespoons tahini (sesame seed paste)
- 2 cloves garlic, minced
- 4 tablespoons Dijon mustard
- Salt to taste
- Pepper to taste
- 2 cans (6 ounces each) of tuna in water, drained
- 2 medium carrots, chopped

DIRECTIONS:

1. Place the chickpeas in the food processor bowl. Give short pulses until they are broken down into smaller pieces.
2. Transfer the chickpeas to a bowl. Add carrot, celery, garlic, cilantro, tuna, and onion, and mix well.
3. Place the lettuce leaves on a serving platter. Divide the tuna mixture equally and place it over the lettuce leaves.
4. Wrap and serve.

SALMON AND SPINACH PASTA

Servings: 4

NUTRITIONAL VALUES PER SERVING:
¼ recipe
Calories: 453
Fat: 24 g
Carbohydrate: 25 g
Protein: 33 g

INGREDIENTS:
- 1 pound boneless, skinless salmon
- 3 tablespoons butter
- 6 cups chopped spinach
- ⅛ cup grated parmesan cheese
- ⅛ cup chopped fresh parsley
- 2 cups penne pasta
- 2 small onions, chopped
- ½ cup low-fat sour cream
- 2 cloves garlic, minced
- Salt to taste
- Pepper to taste

DIRECTIONS:
1. Follow the directions given on the package of pasta and cook the pasta.
2. While the pasta is cooking, place a pan over medium heat on another burner.
3. Add butter. When butter melts, add onion and cook until onion is soft.
4. Stir in the salmon. Cook until the fish flakes easily when pierced with a fork.
5. Add the spinach and stir. Let the spinach wilt for a few minutes.
6. Stir in salt, pepper, garlic, Parmesan, and sour cream. Add pasta and parsley and give it a good stir.
7. Heat thoroughly and serve.

TURKEY AND APRICOT WRAPS

Servings: 2

NUTRITIONAL VALUES PER SERVING:
1 wrap
Calories: 312
Fat: 10 g
Carbohydrate: 33 g
Protein: 20 g

INGREDIENTS:
- ¼ cup reduced-fat cream cheese
- 2 whole-wheat tortillas (8 inches each) at room temperature
- 1 cup fresh arugula or baby spinach
- 1 ½ tablespoons apricot preserves
- 4 ounces deli turkey, sliced

DIRECTIONS:
1. Add cream cheese, and apricot preserves into a bowl and mix well. Divide the mixture equally and spread it over the tortillas, leaving a ½ inch border around the edges.
2. Place turkey slices and arugula on one of the ends. Start rolling from the filling end to the opposite end. Place on a plate with the seam side down.
3. You can serve it right away or chill and serve it later. If you want to serve it chilled, keep it covered in the refrigerator.

SPINACH AND MUSHROOM FRITTATA

Servings: 4

NUTRITIONAL VALUES PER SERVING:
1 wedge
Calories: 282
Fat: 21 g
Carbohydrate: 3 g
Protein: 20 g

INGREDIENTS:
- 4 tablespoons avocado oil or any cooking oil
- 2 cups sliced spinach
- 1 cup shredded low-fat mozzarella cheese
- 2 cups sliced white mushrooms
- 6 large eggs, beaten
- Salt to taste
- Pepper to taste

DIRECTIONS:
1. Preheat the oven to 400° F.
2. Place an ovenproof skillet over high heat. Add 2 tablespoons of oil to the skillet and let it heat.
3. Meanwhile, add salt and pepper to the beaten eggs and whisk well.
4. Add half the cheese and whisk well.

5. When the oil is hot, add mushrooms and stir. Cook for a few minutes until the moisture is released. Stir in the spinach. Cook for about a minute. Spread the mixture all over the skillet.
6. Drizzle the egg mixture all over the vegetables in the skillet. Do not stir. Let the frittata cook for about 3 to 4 minutes.
7. Turn off the heat. Shift the skillet into the oven. Make sure to wear oven mitts.
8. Set the timer for about 5 minutes and bake.
9. Now set the oven to broil mode and broil for 1 to 2 minutes or until golden brown on top.
10. Take the skillet from the oven and let it cool for about 10 minutes.
11. Cut into 4 equal wedges and serve.

PINEAPPLE FRIED RICE

Servings: 3

NUTRITIONAL VALUES PER SERVING:
1/3 recipe
Calories: 145
Fat: 8 g
Carbohydrate: 57 g
Protein: 10 g

INGREDIENTS:
- ½ tablespoon cooking oil of your choice
- ½ medium red bell pepper, diced
- 1 stalk green onion, sliced
- ½ cup pineapple tidbits
- 4 tablespoons low-sodium soy sauce
- 2 teaspoons sugar
- 4 chicken apple sausage links, chopped
- 4 medium carrots, diced
- 4 cups cooked brown rice
- 1/3 cup chopped cilantro
- 2 teaspoons lime juice

DIRECTIONS:

1. Place a large pan or wok over medium-high heat. Add oil to the pan and let it heat.
2. Add sausage and stir. Cook for a few minutes until light brown. Stir every 2 to 3 minutes.
3. Stir in the carrots and bell peppers and cook for a few minutes until they are slightly tender, but they should have the crunch.
4. In the meantime, add soy sauce, lime juice, and sugar into a bowl and whisk well.
5. Pour the mixture into the pan and mix well. Stir in rice, cilantro, pineapple, and scallions.
6. Heat thoroughly.
7. You can use leftover brown rice or even white rice. If you are making the rice yourself, follow the instructions given on the package and cook the rice.
8. Divide the pineapple fried rice into 3 plates and serve.

BANANA ROLL-UPS

Servings: 2

NUTRITIONAL VALUES PER SERVING:
1 banana roll without serving options
Calories:
Fat: g
Carbohydrate: g
Protein: g

INGREDIENTS:
- 2 whole-wheat tortillas (8 inches each) at room temperature
- 4 tablespoons natural peanut butter
- 2 teaspoons honey
- 2 medium bananas, peeled (leave them whole)
- Serving options:
- 8 strawberries, sliced
- ½ cup pretzels
- 1 stalk celery, cut into pieces

DIRECTIONS:
1. If you do not have natural peanut butter, you can use regular peanut butter but do not add the honey.
2. Combine peanut butter and honey in a bowl. Spread half of the peanut butter mixture on each tortilla. Place a banana along the diameter of a tortilla. Do this with the other banana and tortilla as well.
3. Fold the tortilla's bottom edge over the banana. Next, fold the sides inwards from the ends of the banana.
4. 4. Continue to roll until you get to the other end.
5. Serve this with strawberry, celery, and pretzels if using. This will be a complete meal.
6. You can use this as a snack as well. Cut the roll into about 1-inch pieces crosswise and serve.

BEEF FAJITAS

Servings: 4

NUTRITIONAL VALUES PER SERVING:
2 fajitas
Calories: 412
Fat: 19 g
Carbohydrate: 24 g
Protein: 35 g

INGREDIENTS:
- 1 pound steak, cut into ½-inch thick strips
- 2 large bell peppers of any color or use a mixture
- Juice of 2 lemons
- 2 tablespoons olive oil
- 2 small onions, sliced
- 6 tablespoons soy sauce
- 2 teaspoons chili powder (or use lesser if you do not prefer it hot)
- 8 small corn tortillas

DIRECTIONS:
1. Add soy sauce, chili powder, lemon juice, and oil into a bowl and stir.
2. Place bell peppers and onions in a bowl. Drizzle some of the sauce mixtures over the bell peppers and stir.
3. Add steak into the remaining sauce mixture and stir. Keep the bowls aside for 20 minutes. You are marinating the steak and vegetables.
4. Place a skillet over medium heat. Add the meat and cook until the meat is brown on the underside. Flip sides and cook the other side of the steak strips until brown. Transfer the meat to a bowl.
5. Add the marinated vegetables into the skillet and cook for a few minutes until tender.
6. Add the steak into the skillet and give the mixture a good stir.
7. Distribute the meat and vegetables equally among the tortillas. Wrap and serve.

MEATLESS HAMBURGER

Servings: 4

NUTRITIONAL VALUES PER SERVING:
1 hamburger
Calories: 258
Fat: 10.63 g
Carbohydrate: 34.6 g
Protein: 10 g

INGREDIENTS:
- 4 whole-meal burger buns
- 2 bell peppers, finely chopped
- 1 plum tomato, chopped
- 2 tablespoons olive oil
- ½ teaspoon salt
- 1 cup cottage cheese, finely chopped
- 1 onion, chopped
- ¼ cup chopped parsley
- 2 teaspoons dried herbs mix

DIRECTIONS:
1. Pour oil into a pan. Place the pan over medium heat. When the oil is hot, add onion and stir. Cook until they are soft. Stir often.
2. Stir in the bell pepper, tomatoes, dried herbs, parsley, and salt. Turn down the heat and let it cook over low heat until the bell pepper and tomatoes are soft.
3. Stir in cottage cheese. Cook for another 5 minutes.
4. Remove the mixture into a bowl.
5. Now split the buns and toast them in batches in the pan until brown on either side.
6. Spread the cottage cheese mixture on the bottom half of the buns. Cover with the top half of the buns and serve.

SPICY CHICKEN BURGER

Servings: 2

NUTRITIONAL VALUES PER SERVING:
1 chicken burger with ½ sweet potato
Calories: 345
Fat: 7 g
Carbohydrate: 40 g
Protein: 34 g

INGREDIENTS:
- ½ pound ground chicken breast
- ½ teaspoon chopped chipotle pepper in adobo sauce
- ⅛ teaspoon salt or to taste 1/2 teaspoon olive oil or any cooking oil
- 2 lettuce leaves
- 2 whole-grain or potato slider buns, split
- 2 large tomato slices
- 1 teaspoon grated onion
- ½ teaspoon ground cumin
- White of a small egg
- Fries of 1 medium sweet potato

DIRECTIONS:
1. *To make the burger:* Add ground chicken, chipotle pepper, salt, egg white, cumin, and onion into a bowl and stir until well combined.
2. Divide the mixture into 2 equal portions and shape them into balls. Flatten the balls to shape like burgers.
3. Pour oil into a nonstick pan. Place the pan over medium-high heat. Swirl the pan to spread the oil. Place the burgers in the pan. Cook for about 4 to 5 minutes. Flip the burgers over and cook the other side for 4 to 5 minutes or until cooked through inside.
4. *To assemble:* Toast the burger buns if desired. Place a lettuce leaf and a tomato slice on the bottom half of each bun. Place a burger on each. Serve with the bun's top half on top.
5. To make fries, refer to the Chapter on Side Dish Recipes.

PAN SEARED STEAK WITH GARLIC BUTTER

Servings: 2

NUTRITIONAL VALUES PER SERVING:
½ steak
Calories: 542
Fat: 40 g
Carbohydrate: 1 g
Protein: 46 g

INGREDIENTS:
- 1 New York strip steak or Ribeye or sirloin steak (about 1 pound)
- ¾ teaspoon sea salt
- Oil to brush
- ½ teaspoon freshly ground black pepper
- 1 clove garlic, peeled, quartered
- 1 tablespoon unsalted butter
- 1 teaspoon sliced fresh rosemary

DIRECTIONS:
1. Dry the steak by patting it with paper towels. Brush the steak with oil. Sprinkle salt and pepper over the steak.
2. *How to cook a steak:* Place a skillet over medium-high heat and let it heat.
3. Place the steak in the skillet.
4. *For rare*: Cook for 2-3 minutes. Flip the side once and cook the other side for 2-3 minutes. Press the steak in the center using a pair of tongs (back part). If it is soft, it is ready.

5. *For medium:* Cook for 4 minutes. Flip the side once and cook the other side for 4 minutes. Using a pair of tongs (back part), press the steak in the center. If it is slightly firmer, it is ready.

6. *For well cooked:* Cook for 5-6 minutes. Flip the side once and cook the other side for 5-6 minutes. Press the steak in the center using a pair of tongs (back part). If it is very firm, it is ready.

7. When the steak is cooked, as you like, turn the heat low.

8. Add butter, rosemary, and garlic to the pan. Mix well. Once the butter melts, pick the melted butter mixture with a spoon and drizzle over the steak. Cook for 1 minute. Flip the sides and drizzle the butter sauce over the steak. Cook for 1 minute.

9. Remove the steak from the pan and place it on a plate. Cover the steak with foil and allow it to rest for 5 minutes.

10. Slice and serve topped with garlic butter sauce mixed with dripped liquid from the plate.

CHAPTER 6

DINNER RECIPES

P.F. CHANG'S STYLE MONGOLIAN BEEF

Servings: 8

NUTRITIONAL VALUES PER SERVING:
Without rice or noodles
Calories: 342
Fat: 8 g
Carbohydrate: 40 g
Protein: 28 g

INGREDIENTS:
- 5 ½ tablespoons vegetable oil or olive oil
- 8 cloves garlic, peeled, finely minced
- ½ cup water
- 2 pounds flank steak, cut into ¼-inch thick slices
- 4 green onions, sliced
- 1 teaspoon minced ginger
- 1 cup soy sauce, preferably low-sodium
- 1 cup packed brown sugar
- ⅔ cup cornstarch
- Cooked rice or noodles to serve

DIRECTIONS:
1. You can freeze the steak for about an hour before slicing. It makes the slicing easier.
2. Pour 1 tablespoon of oil into a pan. Place the pan over medium-low heat. When the oil is hot, add garlic and ginger and stir for about 30 seconds until you get a nice aroma.

3. Stir in water, soy sauce, and brown sugar. Cook until a bit thick, stirring often. Turn off the heat.
4. Sprinkle cornstarch over the steak and toss well.
5. Place a wok over a medium-high flame. Pour about a tablespoon of oil and wait for the oil to heat up. Add some of the beef into the wok and cook for about a couple of minutes (need not cook it fully). Remove the beef onto a plate.
6. Cook the remaining beef in batches using a tablespoon of oil each time (previous step).
7. Add the cooked beef to the sauce. Place the pan over medium heat and give the mixture a good stir. Heat thoroughly, stirring often.
8. Add green onions and stir.
9. Serve beef over rice or noodles.

HERBED PORK CHOPS

Servings: 2

NUTRITIONAL VALUES PER SERVING:
1 pork chop
Calories: 154
Fat: 6 g
Carbohydrate: 1 g
Protein: 22 g

INGREDIENTS:
- 2 boneless pork loin chops (4 ounces each)
- 1 tablespoon chopped fresh parsley
- ¼ teaspoon dried thyme, crushed
- ¼ teaspoon dried rosemary, crushed
- ⅛ teaspoon pepper
- Cooking oil spray

DIRECTIONS:
1. Drizzle lemon juice over the pork chops.
2. Add the herbs and pepper into a bowl and mix well.
3. Sprinkle this mixture over the pork chops and rub it into the meat.
4. Preheat the oven to 400° F.
5. Place an ovenproof skillet over high heat. Spray the pan with some cooking spray.
6. When the pan is hot, place the pork chops and cook for 3 – 4 minutes or until the underside is brown. Flip sides and cook for 3 – 4 minutes or until the underside is brown. Turn off the heat.
7. Shift the skillet into the oven. Bake for about 6 – 8 minutes or until the internal temperature of the meat in the thickest part shows 145° F on the meat thermometer (insert a meat thermometer in the thickest part of the meat).
8. Rest the meat for 5 minutes and serve.

PAN SEARED CHICKEN BREASTS

Servings: 2

NUTRITIONAL VALUES PER SERVING:
1 chicken breast
Calories: 254
Fat: 10 g
Carbohydrate: 13 g
Protein: 25 g

INGREDIENTS:
- 2 chicken breasts
- Kosher salt to taste
- ½ teaspoon garlic powder
- 1 teaspoon Italian seasoning
- ¼ cup all-purpose flour
- ½ tablespoon coconut oil or olive oil
- Freshly ground pepper to taste
- Paprika to taste (optional)

DIRECTIONS:
1. Place a stainless steel or cast–iron skillet over medium heat. Add oil and let the pan heat.
2. To obtain an equal thickness, use a meat mallet to pound the chicken breast. Everywhere should be thin.
3. Italian seasoning, garlic powder, salt, and pepper are used to season the chicken.
4. Place flour on a plate. Dredge the chicken breasts in the flour on both sides.
5. Place chicken in the skillet. Do not stir or move the chicken around.
6. Cook for 2-3 minutes without covering. Cook until golden brown and the fat is released. Flip sides and cook for 2-3 minutes.
7. Take out chicken from the pan and use it as required. You can serve it over pasta, with vegetables, or with any side dish of your choice.

MEDITERRANEAN CHICKEN

Servings: 1

NUTRITIONAL VALUES PER SERVING:
½ recipe
Calories: 336
Fat: 18 g
Carbohydrate: 6 g
Protein: 36 g

INGREDIENTS:
- 2 boneless, skinless chicken breast halves
- ⅛ teaspoon pepper
- 1 cup grape tomatoes
- 1 ½ tablespoons capers, drained
- ⅛ teaspoon salt
- 1 ½ tablespoons olive oil
- 8 pitted Greek or ripe olives, sliced

DIRECTIONS:
1. Preheat the oven to 475° F.
2. Pour oil into an ovenproof skillet. Place the skillet over medium heat. Let the oil heat.
3. Place the chicken in the heated oil after seasoning with salt and pepper. Cook for approximately two to three minutes, or until golden brown on the bottom. The chicken should be cooked for two to three minutes on the other side. Turn off the heat.
4. Stir in the olives, tomatoes, and capers. Shift the skillet into the oven.
5. Bake for ten to fifteen minutes, or until well done. The interior temperature of the meat should read 165° F on the meat thermometer when it is fully cooked. To check the temperature, use a meat thermometer in the area of the flesh that is the thickest.
6. Serve hot.

CRANBERRY BALSAMIC CHICKEN THIGHS

Servings: 2

NUTRITIONAL VALUES PER SERVING:
1 thigh with 3 tablespoons of cranberry sauce
Calories: 317
Fat: 17.7 g
Carbohydrate: 16 g
Protein: 22.6 g

INGREDIENTS:
- 2 bone-in chicken thighs
- ⅛ teaspoon pepper
- ¾ cup fresh or frozen cranberries (defrosted if frozen)
- 1 tablespoon honey
- ¼ teaspoon salt, divided
- ½ tablespoon extra-virgin olive oil
- 2 tablespoons balsamic vinegar
- ½ teaspoon finely chopped thyme + extra to garnish

DIRECTIONS:
1. Pour oil into a skillet and place the skillet over medium-high heat.
2. Season the chicken with pepper and half the salt. With the skin side facing down, put the chicken in the skillet.
3. Turn down the heat to medium. Cook for 6 – 7 minutes or until the underside is golden brown. Do not disturb the chicken during this time. Retain about ½ tablespoon of fat in the pan and drain the remaining fat.
4. Flip the sides of the chicken. Stir in vinegar, thyme, cranberries, and honey.

5. When the mixture starts simmering, bring down the heat. Cover the skillet partially and cook until the internal temperature of the meat in the thickest part shows 165° F on the meat thermometer.

6. Remove the chicken from the pan using a slotted spoon and place it in a serving dish.

7. Turn up the heat to high heat and stir in the remaining salt. Simmer for about a minute or until the sauce is thick.

8. Serve hot.

CREAMY CHICKEN AND MUSHROOMS

Servings: 2

NUTRITIONAL VALUES PER SERVING:
1 cutlet with ¼ heaping cup of sauce
Calories: 325
Fat: 19.6 g
Carbohydrate: 4.2 g
Protein: 29.1 g

INGREDIENTS:
- 2 chicken cutlets (4 – 5 ounces each)
- ¼ cup dry white wine
- 1 tablespoon finely chopped fresh parsley
- 2 cups sliced, mixed mushrooms
- ¼ cup heavy cream
- 1 tablespoon canola oil or any cooking oil
- ¼ teaspoon pepper
- ¼ teaspoon salt

DIRECTIONS:
1. Pour ½ tablespoon of oil into a skillet. Place the skillet over medium-high heat. Season the chicken with half the pepper and half the salt. Place the chicken in the skillet.
2. Turn down the heat to medium. Cook for 3 – 4 minutes or until the underside is golden brown. Do not disturb the chicken during this time.
3. Flip the sides of the chicken. Cook for 3 – 4 minutes.
4. Remove the chicken onto a plate.

5. Pour ½ tablespoon of oil into the skillet. When the oil is hot, add mushrooms and mix well. Soon the mushrooms will release some of their liquid. Cook until the liquid evaporates.
6. Add the remaining salt and pepper along with the cream and any chicken juices from the plate of chicken.
7. Mix well and add the chicken to the pan. Stir until the sauce coats the chicken. Heat thoroughly and turn off the heat.
8. Garnish with parsley and serve.

HEALTHY LASAGNA

Servings: 3

NUTRITIONAL VALUES PER SERVING:
1/3 recipe
Calories: 273
Fat: 8.7 g
Carbohydrate: 18.7 g
Protein: 27 g

INGREDIENTS:
- ½ pound Italian seasoned ground turkey or regular ground turkey or ground chicken or ground lean beef
- ¾ cup fat-free cottage cheese
- ½ teaspoon Italian seasoning
- ½ heaping cup of shredded low-fat mozzarella cheese
- 1 cup marinara sauce
- ⅛ cup shredded parmesan cheese
- 3 no-boil lasagna noodles (also called as oven ready lasagna noodles)
- Finely chopped fresh parsley to garnish (optional)

DIRECTIONS:
1. Add turkey into a skillet. Place the skillet over medium heat. Cook until brown all over. Stir often. As you stir, break the meat into crumbles.
2. Add marinara sauce and stir. Keep it aside for now.
3. Add cottage cheese, Italian seasoning, and Parmesan cheese into a mixing bowl and mix well.
4. Preheat the oven to 350° F. Take a small, square, or rectangular baking dish and grease it with some cooking oil spray.

5. Cover the bottom of the baking dish with a thin coating of the beef sauce. Place a layer of lasagna noodles over the sauce. Next, spread half the cottage cheese mixture. Repeat the layers once again.
6. Spread the remaining meat sauce on top of the cheese mixture. Finally, sprinkle mozzarella cheese on top.
7. The dish's top should be covered with aluminum foil. Put the baking dish into the oven and set the timer for 30 minutes.
8. Remove the foil after 20 minutes and bake for the remaining time.
9. Take out the baking dish and let it sit for 10 minutes.
10. Divide into 3 equal parts and serve.

PIZZA

Servings: 4

NUTRITIONAL VALUES PER SERVING:
1 wedge without a side dish
Calories: 180
Fat: 8.3 g
Carbohydrate: 16.2 g
Protein: 12.2 g

INGREDIENTS:

For the seasoned ground turkey:
- ½ pound extra-lean ground turkey
- 1 tablespoon chopped fresh oregano
- 2 cloves garlic, peeled, chopped, or minced
- ¼ teaspoon kosher salt

For the pizza:
- ½ pound whole-wheat pizza dough
- ½ tablespoon hemp seeds
- 4 – 5 fresh basil leaves, torn
- 2 small cloves garlic, peeled, minced
- ¼ large red bell pepper, deseeded, thinly sliced
- ¼ cup unsalted tomato sauce
- 1 teaspoon nutritional yeast
- 1 tablespoon chopped fresh oregano
- ½ cup seasoned ground turkey
- ¼ large green bell pepper, deseeded, thinly sliced
- 1 small tomato, thinly sliced
- Crushed red pepper flakes to taste
- 1 small onion, thinly sliced
- ½ cup grated fresh mozzarella cheese
- Cooking oil spray

DIRECTIONS:

1. *To make seasoned turkey:* Spray a skillet with some cooking oil spray. Place the skillet over medium-high heat.
2. Add garlic, turkey, salt, and oregano when the skillet is hot and stir. As you stir, break the meat into smaller pieces.
3. Cook until the temperature of the meat is 165° F. Turn off the heat. Use ½ cup of seasoned turkey to make the pizza. The remaining meat can be stored in the refrigerator or frozen and used in another recipe.
4. *To assemble the pizza:* Preheat oven to 400° F. Spray a small cast-iron pan or pizza pan (about 6 – 7 inches) with some cooking oil spray.
5. Place the dough in the prepared skillet and spread it evenly on the bottom, pressing on the edges of the crust.
6. Spoon the tomato sauce on the crust and spread it evenly, leaving about ½ inch border. Scatter hemp seeds, oregano, basil, garlic, and nutritional yeast all over the sauce.
7. Spread ground turkey over the sauce. Place bell pepper, tomato, and onion slices all over the turkey layer.
8. Sprinkle cheese on top. Finally, sprinkle red pepper flakes over the cheese.
9. Place the pan in the oven and set the timer for 25 to 30 minutes or until crisp around the edges.
10. Take out the pan and let it cool for 3–4 minutes. Cut into four equal wedges and serve with a salad or any side dish if desired.

SESAME-TOFU FRIED RICE

Servings: 4

NUTRITIONAL VALUES PER SERVING:
¼ recipe
Calories: 453
Fat: 26 g
Carbohydrate: 43 g
Protein: 13 g

INGREDIENTS:
- 1 package (6 ounces) of extra-firm tofu
- 1 tablespoon maple syrup
- 2 tablespoons low-sodium soy sauce
- 1 cup frozen peas
- 1 cup frozen carrots
- 2 large eggs, beaten
- ½ cup chopped scallions
- 6 tablespoons sesame oil
- 1 tablespoon apple cider vinegar
- 1 tablespoon sesame seeds
- 2 small onions, chopped
- 2 cups cooked white rice
- Salt to taste
- Pepper to taste
- Cooking oil spray

DIRECTIONS:

1. Remove excess moisture from the tofu: For this, line a plate with 2 layers of paper towels. Place tofu over the paper towels. Place 2 layers of paper towels over the tofu. Now place something heavy over the tofu, like a cold drink can or a can of beans.
2. Let it remain like this for about 15 minutes.
3. Remove the papers and chop the tofu into 1-inch cubes.
4. Preheat the oven to 425° F. Put parchment paper on a baking pan to prepare it.
5. Add 1 tablespoon of soy sauce, maple syrup, sesame seeds, vinegar, and 3 tablespoons of sesame oil into a bowl. Stir until well combined.
6. Stir in the tofu. Now spread the tofu on the baking sheet. Set the oven's timer for 40 minutes and place the baking sheet inside. Make sure to stir the tofu every 15 minutes.
7. During the last 10 minutes of baking, place a pan over medium heat. Spray the pan with some cooking oil spray.
8. Add onions and cook for a couple of minutes. Add carrots and peas and cook for 3 – 4 minutes.
9. Add eggs, salt, and pepper and mix well. Stir often until the eggs are soft-cooked.
10. Add the rice, tofu, 1 tablespoon of soy sauce, and remaining sesame oil and mix well. Heat thoroughly.
11. Divide the fried rice into 4 plates and serve.

BLACK BEAN FAJITA SKILLET

Servings: 4

NUTRITIONAL VALUES PER SERVING:
About 2 cups
Calories: 310
Fat: 8 g
Carbohydrate: 47 g
Protein: 14 g

INGREDIENTS:
- 2 tablespoons olive oil
- 2 cans (15 ounces each) of unsalted black beans, rinsed
- ½ teaspoon salt (to be added if the Southwest seasoning blend is unsalted)
- 2 packages (12 ounces each) of sliced fajita vegetables (with onions and bell peppers)
- 1 teaspoon Southwest-style seasoning blend
- ½ cup shredded cheddar cheese

DIRECTIONS:
1. Pour oil into a large skillet. Place the skillet over medium heat. When the oil is hot, add the fajita vegetables and stir. The vegetables should be cooked for a few minutes until they are crisp and slightly tender.
2. Add salt, seasoning blend, and black beans and stir. Heat thoroughly.
3. Distribute the vegetable mixture among 4 bowls. Scatter 2 tablespoons of cheese on top, on each bowl, and serve.

BAKED EGGS IN TOMATO SAUCE WITH KALE

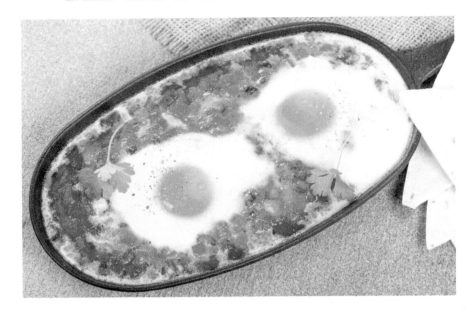

Servings: 2

NUTRITIONAL VALUES PER SERVING:
2 eggs with 1 cup of sauce, without bread
Calories: 344
Fat: 20.3 g
Carbohydrate: 20.6 g
Protein: 21.4 g

INGREDIENTS:
- ½ tablespoon extra-virgin olive oil
- ¼ teaspoon salt, divided
- ½ jar (from a 25 ounces jar) of marinara sauce or 1 ½ cups of tomato sauce
- 1 ½ packages (10 ounces each) of frozen chopped kale, drained, squeezed of excess moisture
- Pepper to taste
- 4 large eggs

DIRECTIONS:
1. Pour oil into a skillet. Place the skillet over medium heat. Add kale, pepper, and ⅛ teaspoon salt when the oil is hot. Mix well.
2. Cook for a couple of minutes. Add tomato sauce and mix well. When the sauce starts simmering, turn down the heat to low.
3. Make 4 cavities in the sauce at different spots. Crack an egg into each cavity. Sprinkle the remaining salt over the eggs. Sprinkle some pepper as well.
4. Cover the skillet and cook until the whites are set, and the yolks are slightly runny.
5. Serve hot with bread or dinner rolls if desired.

PESTO RAVIOLI WITH SPINACH AND TOMATOES

Servings: 2

NUTRITIONAL VALUES PER SERVING:
1-½ cups
Calories: 361
Fat: 18.6 g
Carbohydrate: 35.2 g
Protein: 13.8 g

INGREDIENTS:

- 1 package (8 ounces) of frozen or refrigerated cheese ravioli
- 1 cup grape tomatoes
- 3 – 4 tablespoons pesto
- ½ tablespoon olive oil
- 2.5 ounces of baby spinach

DIRECTIONS:

1. Follow the directions given on the package of ravioli and cook it.
2. Pour oil into a nonstick pan. Place the pan over medium heat. When the oil is hot, stir the tomatoes into the oil.
3. Cook for a few minutes until slightly soft. After one to two minutes, add the spinach and stir.
4. Fold the ravioli and pesto into the spinach mixture.
5. Serve.

SPINACH AND TOMATO PASTA

Servings: 2

NUTRITIONAL VALUES PER SERVING:
½ recipe
Calories: 333
Fat: 7.1 g
Carbohydrate: 55 g
Protein: 15 g

INGREDIENTS:
- ½ tablespoon olive oil
- 3 cloves garlic, finely chopped
- ¾ cup unsalted chicken stock
- 4 ounces whole grain spaghetti or linguine
- 5 ounces of fresh spinach
- ½ cup chopped onion
- ½ can (from a 14.5-ounce can) of unsalted petite diced tomatoes with their liquid
- ¼ teaspoon dried oregano
- ¼ teaspoon salt
- ⅛ cup grated parmesan cheese

DIRECTIONS:
1. Pour oil into a Dutch oven or heavy saucepan. Place the Dutch oven over medium-high heat.
2. When the oil is hot, add onion and stir. Cook for a couple of minutes. Stir in the garlic and cook for a few minutes until the onion is light brown.
3. Stir in the oregano, stock, and tomatoes. When the mixture starts boiling, stir in the spaghetti.
4. Press the spaghetti into the liquid in the pot. When the pasta is al dente, reduce the heat to medium-low.
5. Add salt and spinach and stir. Heat thoroughly and turn off the heat. Let it rest for 5 minutes.
6. Garnish with cheese and serve.

LEMON SALMON WITH BASIL

Servings: 2

NUTRITIONAL VALUES PER SERVING:
1 salmon fillet
Calories: 294
Fat: 18 g
Carbohydrate: 3 g
Protein: 29 g

INGREDIENTS:
- 2 salmon filets (6 ounces each)
- ½ tablespoons grated lemon zest
- ⅛ teaspoon pepper
- 1 medium lemon, thinly sliced
- 1 teaspoon olive oil
- ¼ teaspoon salt
- 1 tablespoon thinly sliced fresh basil leaves + extra to garnish
- Cooking oil spray

DIRECTIONS:
1. Set the oven to 375 degrees F. Cooking spray should be used to coat a baking pan.Lay the salmon filets in the pan. Pour ½ teaspoon of oil over each filet. Season with salt, pepper, and lemon zest. Scatter basil on top.
2. Slices of lemon should be placed above the fish. Set the timer for 15 to 20 minutes in the oven, or until the mixture easily flakes when tested with a fork. Place the baking pan in the oven.
3. Garnish with some basil and serve.

CHAPTER 7

SIDE DISH
RECIPES

HONEY-GARLIC BRUSSELS SPROUTS

Servings: 3

NUTRITIONAL VALUES PER SERVING:
⅔ cup
Calories: 100
Fat: 3 g
Carbohydrate: 18 g
Protein: 5 g

INGREDIENTS:
- 1 pound Brussels sprouts, trimmed, halved
- ½ tablespoon lemon juice
- 1 teaspoon garlic salt
- 1 tablespoon honey
- ½ tablespoon olive oil

DIRECTIONS:
1. 1. Set the oven temperature to 425°F. Line a baking pan with aluminum foil to prepare it.
2. Place Brussels sprouts in the baking pan. Add lemon juice, garlic salt, honey, and oil over the Brussels sprouts and toss well. Spread it evenly in the pan.
3. Put the baking sheet in the oven, and set the timer for 15 to 20 minutes, or until the cookies are soft inside and lightly browned on the exterior. Make sure to stir the Brussels sprouts after about 10 minutes of baking.
4. Mix well and serve.

BAKED SWEET POTATO FRIES

Servings: 4

NUTRITIONAL VALUES PER SERVING:
¼ recipe
Calories: 122
Fat: 4.8 g
Carbohydrate: 18.7 g
Protein: 1.8 g

INGREDIENTS:
- 2 large sweet potatoes, peeled, cut into wedges
- ½ teaspoon salt
- 4 teaspoons canola oil
- ¼ teaspoon cayenne pepper
- Herbs or spices of your choice to taste (optional)

DIRECTIONS:
1. Set the oven's temperature to 425°F. A baking sheet with a rim can be lined with aluminum foil.
2. Place the sweet potato wedges in a bowl. Drizzle oil over the wedges. Sprinkle salt, cayenne pepper, and any other seasonings if using, and mix well.
3. Arrange the slices on the prepared baking sheet, then bake it. Set the timer for about 20 minutes or until brown outside and cooked through inside.
4. Turn the wedges over after about 10 – 12 minutes of baking.
5. Divide into 4 equal portions and serve.

CHEESE AND GARLIC BISCUITS

Servings: 15

NUTRITIONAL VALUES PER SERVING:
1 biscuit
Calories: 81
Fat: 5 g
Carbohydrate: 7 g
Protein: 2 g

INGREDIENTS:
- 1 ¼ cups biscuit or baking mix
- ½ teaspoon garlic powder
- ½ cup buttermilk
- 6 tablespoons shredded sharp cheddar cheese
- ½ teaspoon salad dressing mix

For the topping:
- ¼ cup butter, melted
- ¼ teaspoon garlic powder
- ⅛ teaspoon pepper
- ½ tablespoon minced chives
- ¼ teaspoon ranch salad dressing mix
- Cooking oil spray

DIRECTIONS:
1. Set the oven's temperature to 450° F. Spray cooking oil on a baking sheet to grease it.
2. Add baking mix, garlic powder, cheese, and ranch salad dressing mix into a bowl and stir until well combined.
3. Add buttermilk and stir until just combined, making sure not to over-mix.

4. Take a tablespoonful of the batter and drop it on the prepared baking sheet. Repeat this process with the remaining batter. Make sure to leave a gap between the biscuits.
5. Place the baking sheet in the oven and set the timer for 6 to 8 minutes or until golden brown.
6. In the meantime, prepare the topping: Add melted butter, garlic powder, pepper, chives, and dressing mix into a small bowl and stir well.
7. Brush this mixture over the baked biscuits. Before serving, let the biscuits cool for a few minutes.

HONEY GARLIC BUTTER ROASTED CARROTS

Servings: 3

NUTRITIONAL VALUES PER SERVING:
1/3 recipe
Calories: 281
Fat: 15 g
Carbohydrate: 35 g
Protein: 2 g

INGREDIENTS:
- 1 pound carrots, trimmed, peeled if desired, cut into thirds
- 1 ½ tablespoons honey
- ⅛ teaspoon salt or to taste
- 1 tablespoon chopped fresh parsley
- 3 tablespoons butter
- 2 cloves garlic, peeled, minced
- Cracked pepper to taste

DIRECTIONS:
1. Set the oven temperature to 425°F. Spray some cooking oil on a baking sheet to grease it.
2. Add butter to a pan. Place the pan over medium heat. When butter melts, add honey and stir until it is well combined.
3. Stir in the garlic. Cook for a few seconds until you get a nice aroma.
4. Stir in the carrots and let them simmer for about a minute or until the sauce coats them.
5. Turn off the heat. Spread the carrots on the prepared baking sheet without overlapping.
6. Place the baking sheet in the oven and set the timer for 20 minutes. Stir once halfway through roasting.
7. Set the oven to broil mode. Broil for 2 – 3 minutes. Sprinkle some more salt and pepper if you like, and serve.

CRISPY BAKED FRENCH FRIES

Servings: 2

NUTRITIONAL VALUES PER SERVING:
¼ recipe
Calories: 194
Fat: 4 g
Carbohydrate: 37 g
Protein: 4 g

INGREDIENTS:
- 2 medium russet potatoes, scrubbed, rinsed
- ¼ teaspoon kosher salt
- ½ tablespoon olive oil
- ⅛ teaspoon freshly ground pepper

DIRECTIONS:
1. Preheat the oven to 400° F. Prepare a baking sheet by lining it with parchment paper.
2. To cut the potato into fries: Cut a thin slice from one of the edges of the potato. Place the potato, so the flat part touches your cutting board. Next, cut thin slices lengthwise (depending on how thick you want the fries).
3. Stack 2 to 3 slices together and cut into thin sticks lengthwise if you want long fries or widthwise if you want short fries.
4. Repeat the process with all the potatoes.
5. Drizzle oil over the potatoes. Sprinkle salt and pepper and mix well. Spread the potatoes on the baking sheet.
6. Place the baking sheet in the oven and set the timer for 35 – 40 minutes or until the fries are brown and crisp. Stir the fries every 10 – 12 minutes.
7. Serve hot.

PARMESAN SCALLOPED POTATOES WITH SPINACH

Servings: 5

NUTRITIONAL VALUES PER SERVING:
½ cup
Calories: 212
Fat: 7.4 g
Carbohydrate: 28.4 g
Protein: 9.5 g

INGREDIENTS:
- 1 ¼ pounds Yukon gold potatoes, cut into ¼ inch thick, round slices (about 4 cups)
- ½ cup finely chopped onion
- 1 ½ tablespoons all-purpose flour
- Pepper to taste
- ½ pound chopped, frozen spinach, thawed
- 1 ½ tablespoons extra-virgin olive oil, divided
- 1 clove garlic, minced
- ¼ teaspoon salt
- 1 ¼ cups low-fat milk
- ½ cup grated parmesan cheese, divided

DIRECTIONS:
1. Preheat the oven to 425° F.
2. Place the potato slices in a bowl. Drizzle ½ tablespoon of oil over the potato slices and toss well.
3. Place the potato slices on a baking sheet in a single layer. Bake for about 20 – 25 minutes or until the slices are tender.
4. Pour 1 tablespoon of oil into a saucepan and place it over medium heat. Stir in the onion and cook until golden brown, stirring often.
5. Stir in the garlic. Stir constantly for about 30 seconds.
6. Next, stir in the salt, flour, and pepper. Keep stirring for about a minute.

7. Pour milk and keep on stirring until the sauce is slightly thick. Make sure to scrape the bottom of the saucepan to remove any browned bits that may be stuck.
8. Let it cook for a couple of minutes until the sauce is thick. Turn off the heat and add spinach. Mix well.
9. Turn the oven to broil mode.
10. Place half the potato slices in a baking dish. Spoon half the sauce over the potatoes, spreading it evenly. Sprinkle ¼ cup of cheese.
11. Repeat the previous step once again. For one to two minutes, or when the cheese is melted and faintly browned, place the baking dish in the oven and turn on the broiler.
12. Cool for 8 – 10 minutes and serve.

CHAPTER 8

SNACK
RECIPES

FRUIT SALSA

Servings: 12

NUTRITIONAL VALUES PER SERVING:
¼ cup salsa without tortilla chips
Calories: 48
Fat: 0 g
Carbohydrate: 13 g
Protein: 0 g

INGREDIENTS:
- 2 cans (8 ounces each) of unsweetened crushed pineapple, drained
- ½ cup chopped red onion
- Tortilla chips to serve
- 2 cans (8 ounces each) of mandarin oranges, drained and chopped
- ⅛ cup chopped cilantro

DIRECTIONS:
1. Add fruits, onion, and cilantro into a bowl and stir.
2. Keep the bowl covered in the refrigerator until ready to serve.
3. This is to be served with tortilla chips.

SAVORY CUCUMBER SANDWICHES

Servings: 18

NUTRITIONAL VALUES PER SERVING:
1 sandwich
Calories: 62
Fat: 5 g
Carbohydrate: 4 g
Protein: 1 g

INGREDIENTS:
- 4 ounces cream cheese, softened
- ½ envelope of Italian salad dressing mix
- 18 round cucumber slices
- ¼ cup mayonnaise
- 18 slices snack rye bread
- Chopped fresh dill to garnish (optional)

DIRECTIONS:
1. Add cream cheese, salad dressing mix, and mayonnaise into a bowl and mix until smooth. Cover the bowl and chill for an hour in the refrigerator.
2. Spread a little of this mixture on each of the rye bread slices. Place a cucumber slice on each. Garnish with dill if using and serve.

MINI ZUCCHINI PIZZAS

Servings: 12

NUTRITIONAL VALUES PER SERVING:
1 pizza
Calories: 29
Fat: 2 g
Carbohydrate: 1 g
Protein: 2 g

INGREDIENTS:
- ½ large zucchini, cut into ¼ inch thick slices on the diagonal (12 slices in all)
- Pepper to taste
- 6 tablespoons shredded part-skim mozzarella cheese
- Finely chopped fresh basil to garnish
- Salt to taste
- 3 tablespoons pizza sauce
- ¼ cup mini pepperoni slices

DIRECTIONS:
1. Pre-heat the oven and set it to broil.
2. Grease a baking sheet with some cooking oil spray. On the baking sheet, arrange the zucchini slices in a single layer.
3. Place the baking sheet in the oven, about 3 to 4 inches below the heating element, and broil for 1 to 2 minutes on each side.
4. Season the zucchini with salt and pepper. Spread ½ tablespoon sauce on each zucchini slice, followed by ½ tablespoon cheese. Place pepperoni slices over the cheese and place the baking sheet in the oven.
5. Broil for about 1 minute or until the cheese melts. Garnish with basil and serve.

CRAB PHYLLO CUPS

Servings: 15

NUTRITIONAL VALUES PER SERVING:
1 crab phyllo cup
Calories: 34
Fat: 2 g
Carbohydrate: 3 g
Protein: 1 g

INGREDIENTS:
- ¼ cup reduced-fat spreadable garden vegetable cream cheese
- 6 tablespoons lump crabmeat, drained
- 2 ½ tablespoons chili sauce or to taste
- ¼ teaspoon seafood seasoning
- 1 package (1.9 ounces) of frozen miniature phyllo tart shells

DIRECTIONS:
1. Add cream cheese and seafood seasoning into a bowl and mix well. Add crab and stir gently.
2. Place 2 teaspoons of the crab mixture in each of the tart shells.
3. Drizzle a little chili sauce on top and serve.

STUFFED MINI PEPPERS

Servings: 16

NUTRITIONAL VALUES PER SERVING:
1 stuffed pepper half
Calories: 15
Fat: 0 g
Carbohydrate: 3 g
Protein: 1 g

INGREDIENTS:
- ½ teaspoon cumin seeds
- ⅛ cup chopped cilantro leaves + extra to garnish
- 1 ½ tablespoons cider vinegar
- 8 miniature sweet peppers, cut into 2 halves lengthwise
- ½ can (from 15 ounces can) of chickpeas, rinsed, drained
- 1 ½ tablespoons water
- ⅛ teaspoon salt

DIRECTIONS:
1. Place a small skillet over medium heat. Let the pan dry up and let it become hot.
2. Add cumin seeds and stir until they turn light brown.
3. Turn off the heat and keep stirring for a couple of minutes, so they do not burn.
4. Add chickpeas, cumin seeds, cilantro, vinegar, water, and salt into the food processor bowl. Give short pulses until the mixture is well combined.
5. Fill the mixture into the bell pepper halves. Garnish with cilantro and chill until ready to serve.

CHAPTER 9

DESSERT RECIPES

CLASSIC AMERICAN CHEESECAKE

Servings: 6

NUTRITIONAL VALUES PER SERVING:
1 wedge
Calories: 411.2
Fat: 33.1 g
Carbohydrate: 22 g
Protein: 7.9 g

INGREDIENTS:

For filling:
- 1 pound cream cheese, at room temperature
- ½ teaspoon vanilla extract
- 2 large eggs, lightly beaten
- ½ cup sugar
- ¼ teaspoon salt
- ½ teaspoon finely grated lemon rind

For crust:
- 3 tablespoons butter, unsalted, melted
- 1 ½ tablespoons sugar
- ¾ cup graham cracker crumbs or dry cookie crumbs like gingersnaps

DIRECTIONS:
1. Preheat the oven to 300° F.
2. *To make the crust:* Grease a small (6-inch) springform pan with a little melted butter.

3. Add remaining butter, sugar, and cracker crumbs into a bowl and mix until crumbs are formed.
4. Transfer the crust mixture to the prepared pan. Press it onto the bottom of the pan.
5. Place the springform pan in the oven and bake for 12 – 15 minutes, until light brown.
6. Remove it from the oven and let it to cool.
7. *To make the filling:* Add cream cheese into a mixing bowl, set the electric hand mixer on medium speed, and beat until smooth.
8. Add sugar and beat until creamy. Scrape the sides of the bowl whenever required.
9. Add eggs, vanilla extract, and lemon zest, one ingredient at a time. Beat after adding each ingredient.
10. Spread the filling on the crust.
11. Bake until the edges are set and the center is jiggling. It may take 50-80 minutes.
12. Cool completely. Chill if desired. Cut into 6 equal wedges and serve.

CRISPY PEANUT BUTTER BALLS

Servings: 6

NUTRITIONAL VALUES PER SERVING:
1 ball
Calories: 112
Fat: 7.5 g
Carbohydrate: 8.4 g
Protein: 2.8 g

INGREDIENTS:
- ¼ cup natural peanut butter or almond butter
- ½ teaspoon pure maple syrup
- 6 tablespoons crispy rice cereal
- ¼ cup dark chocolate chips, melted

DIRECTIONS:
1. Take a sheet used for baking and cover it with a sheet of parchment paper.
2. Add peanut butter, maple syrup, and rice cereal into a bowl and stir well.
3. Split the mixture into 6 even parts and roll each one into a ball shape. Lay them on the baking sheet.
4. Place the sheet in the freezer for about 25 – 30 minutes.
5. Melt the chocolate in a microwave-safe bowl, in the microwave for about 30 seconds or until smooth. If it has not melted at 30 seconds, give increments of 10 seconds. Stir every 10 seconds.
6. Dip the balls in melted chocolate, one at a time. Pick it up with a fork and place it on the baking sheet. Freezer for about 15 minutes or until the chocolate hardens.
7. Move the balls into a sealed container that does not allow air to enter, and place it in the refrigerator until you're ready to use them. They can last for about 20 days.

BROWNIES

Servings: 8

NUTRITIONAL VALUES PER SERVING:
1 brownie
Calories: 268
Fat: 14 g
Carbohydrate: 36 g
Protein: 2 g

INGREDIENTS:
- 1 cup white sugar
- ½ cup butter, melted
- ¼ cup cocoa powder
- ¼ teaspoon baking powder
- ¼ cup walnut halves, cut into chunks
- ¾ cup all-purpose flour
- 2 eggs
- ½ teaspoon vanilla extract
- ¼ teaspoon salt

DIRECTIONS:
1. Before you begin, heat your oven to 350° F. Take a small, square baking dish (8 inches) and coat it with cooking spray.Add sugar, cocoa, baking powder, flour, and salt into a bowl and stir well.
2. Stir in the eggs and butter. Stir until the batter is smooth. Do not over-mix.
3. Transfer the batter into the prepared baking dish. Place walnut pieces all over the batter.
4. Put the baking dish in the oven, set the timer for 20 to 25 minutes, and wait until the top is dry and the edges are loose.
5. Cool completely. Cut into 8 equal pieces and serve. To keep any leftover brownies fresh, store them in a sealed container that does not allow air to enter.. It can last for about 10 days if it is refrigerated.

WANT TO KNOW THE 7 PROVEN COOKING STRATEGIES FOR CHEFS?

GET IT NOW!

SIMPLY SCAN THIS QR CODE USING YOUR SMARTPHONE OR TABLET.

CONCLUSION

I want to thank you again for choosing this book! I hope you found it informational and helpful.

Teenage is one of the most important and life-defining phases in life. Different physical and emotional changes accompany it. At this point in life, you start discovering who you are and your place in this world. It is certainly not easy, but it is incredibly exciting too. This is one of those things everyone goes through. During these years, nutrition matters a lot. You must ensure your growing mind and body get all the necessary nutrients. You might have noticed and must be experiencing different changes. This is also a time of growing stress because you are now a step closer to adulthood. However, take a deep breath because this is a fun rollercoaster ride you are on. Make the most of this moment and cherish it. It is also the right time to learn a few skills that will serve you throughout your life. One such skill is cooking.

If you have never cooked or are eager to learn, then there is no time like the present to start. These days, there are more food choices available than ever before. The options are unlimited, from pre packaged and processed foods to frozen dinners, takeout, and fast food. Whoever seldom is, all these things are healthy. Most foods that look like they were mass-produced in a factory are devoid of the nutrition your body needs and are filled with unhealthy things. Also, it is quite expensive to keep to this routine. The good news is that once you start cooking at home, you get complete control over your diet. Eating healthily is not synonymous with eating measly portions or splurging on fancy ingredients. Instead, it is about consciously opting for wholesome and unprocessed ingredients instead of relying on highly processed foods. This is where this book steps into the picture.

Before you can whip up delicious and healthy meals for yourself, your friends, and your family, you must learn a few basic cooking techniques. In this book, you will discover basic cooking techniques that everyone should know. After you become accustomed to it, you will realize how simple and easy cooking is. Forget about spending hours together in the kitchen to cook. It hardly takes any time and effort when you know what to do. Another wonderful benefit of learning to cook is to make you more self-sufficient and independent. These are things that will automatically improve your confidence too. Cooking is a wonderful stressbuster too. If you want to reap all these benefits, going through the information given in this book is the first step.

Now that you have all the information about cooking techniques and different recipes, the next step is to get started. Make a note of all the recipes that strike your fancy, gather the needed ingredients, and follow the simple instructions given. Yes, these are the only three steps you must follow to cook delicious and healthy meals at home within no time. Regardless of whether you know your way around the kitchen or are cooking for the first time, you needn't worry. The recipes given in this book are a great place to begin. Also, they are delicious and healthy. So, you will dig into meals that tickle your taste buds and nourish your body. There is no such thing as starting too early when it comes to eating healthily. The earlier you get started, the better.

After making your way through the recipes in this book, you will feel like a professional chef. Who knows, you might end up with a new hobby too! All this while you are eating healthily. From improving your relationship with food and ensuring your body will get all the nutrients it needs to you learn this essential life skill, cooking at home is something everyone should know how to do. Once you experiment with this book's different recipes and techniques, there is no looking back. You will realize how easy and simple it is to cook delicious meals yourself. The only thing to do is ensure you have all the required ingredients at home and follow the recipes' instructions. So, are you excited to start cooking at home?

If yes, take the first step today and jump into the world of healthy and delicious home-cooked meals with this book!

Thank you, and all the best!

help

Printed in Great Britain
by Amazon

34566868R00071